A Histo
of Sevenoaks

by Janet Davies

First published in Great Britain in 2017
by Oxenhill Books

Designed by Patricia Briggs

Printed by LS1print, www.ls1print.co.uk

ISBN 978-1-0008462-0-6

Contents

Introduction

How much do you know about Sevenoaks?

- Did the Romans settle in Sevenoaks?
- What made Sevenoaks such a prosperous town?
- Why is Knole House known as a calendar house?
- Why did Sevenoaks become 'one oak' for a while?

Read the information on the following pages and you'll be an EXPERT on the history and development of Sevenoaks town.

Let's get started!

From little acorns...
early Sevenoaks

Sevenoaks is the largest town in the Sevenoaks District. Around 25,000 people live there today. But why – and when – did Sevenoaks grow so much bigger than other settlements in the area?

Was it because the Romans came to stay?

No. We know that the Romans weren't *that* interested in settling on the land where Sevenoaks town now lies.

The Romans came to Kent in 43AD, but they didn't choose Sevenoaks, because the land wasn't especially good for farming. The soil was either too sandy, too chalky or too full of flint stones.

Instead, as the Romans started to mix with the local people, they settled further north along the Darent Valley, building farms and holiday homes by the river. The Romans grew wheat here. The land was fertile, it was close to water and it was protected from strong winds by the forests and the sides of the valley. That's why there are now more Roman villa remains in this valley than almost anywhere else in England.

Lullingstone Roman Villa

Lullingstone Roman Villa near Eynsford is one of the most famous and best-preserved Roman sites in Britain. It started off as a farm in around 75AD, and developed over the next four hundred years into a grand residence with a wonderful mosaic floor that we can still admire today.

The mosaic floor at Lullingstone

An added bonus was that the River Darent was much wider and deeper in Roman times than it is today. Farmers could send their produce along this river and then via the River Thames into London. Their goods could be in London in just a couple of days. No wonder the Romans liked this part of the world!

Was it because the Romans could grow vines to make wine in Sevenoaks?

No. The Romans planted vines on the south-facing slopes of the nearby Vale of Holmesdale … but not in Sevenoaks!

The Vale of Holmesdale (or Holmesdale Valley) is the valley to the north of Sevenoaks. It is the dip between Sevenoaks and the North Downs. In today's terms, St John's Hill (the A225) is the road running north, down the valley from Sevenoaks. This leads to the A25, which runs from east to west across the bottom of the valley at Bat and Ball. Then the A225 climbs up once again to the North Downs.

This postcard from the 1950s shows the Holmesdale valley and hills. See how the fields slope down into the sheltered valley and then up again to the North Downs.

SUNDRIDGE FROM CHAPMANS FARM

22100

Has Sevenoaks always been the biggest town around?

No. In the eleventh century Otford was far more important than little old Sevenoaks. Sevenoaks was just one small part of the Great Manor of Otford, looked after through the centuries by the archbishops of Canterbury.

And even in the thirteenth century, Otford was still more important than Sevenoaks. In fact, it was the richest of all the Kent manors held by the archbishops.

The earliest known map of the Sevenoaks area is dated 1355. Otford is shown on the map, but not Sevenoaks!

In medieval times all English land was owned by the king (or queen). Fifty percent of the land was looked after by barons and earls on behalf of the king. They made money from farming and renting out houses, and in return had to fight for their king if he told them to. The king looked after just twenty percent of his property and the rest of the English manors were looked after by the Church. Otford was one of the Church's manors, and covered thirty square miles of land.

Once, the Archbishop's Palace in Otford was as important as Hampton Court in London. There is very little left; this tower is just about all that remains. Henry VIII stayed at Otford with 4,000 of his courtiers in 1520, on his way to the Field of Cloth of Gold. In 1538 he decided that he wanted to own Otford Palace and made Archbishop Thomas Cranmer hand it over to him.

This model of the Archbishop's Palace in Otford shows how it would have looked in the time of Henry VIII. Can you spot the gatehouse?

The Field of Cloth of Gold was a meeting between Henry VIII and Francis I of France. The meeting took place near Calais in 1520 and its purpose was to bring Britain and France together as friends. The two kings did their best to impress each other with lavish costumes decorated with gold, silver and pearls, jousting tournaments, music and feasts, but within two years they were at war.

This is Hampton Court, in London.

Look at the gatehouse towers and compare them with Otford's.

Why Sevenoaks became a settlement

So if the farming was better elsewhere and Otford was more important, why did Sevenoaks eventually become the biggest and busiest town around?

Let's find out why!

Drovers' roads

From Roman times through to the Industrial Revolution, a vast network of drovers' roads developed throughout Britain.

Drovers' roads were tracks used by farmers to move their animals from one place to another. We know that every autumn the farmers up on the North Downs drove their pigs south to the High Weald woodlands around Penshurst. They did this to fatten up their pigs on a feast of acorns and beech nuts. Their journey would have taken them through the area where Sevenoaks now stands. The farmers followed the same route every year, and over time the soft ground wore away to form a well-trodden, sunken track.

Drovers also moved cattle, sheep, turkeys and geese from place to place. They took their animals to markets in towns and cities all over the country.

See if you can spot a drovers' road in the countryside near you. Look for sunken paths like this one, worn down by the drovers and their herds over decades of use.

In a way, the drovers' roads were like the motorways of today. They were wider than other footpaths so that hundreds of animals could be transported in one go.

Drovers' roads were important because there was no other way to get fresh meat to market – don't forget that there were no fridges, freezers or lorries in those days!

The drovers were well paid for their work because they had to keep their animals healthy and under control for very long distances. They also carried news between farms and were trusted with financial payments.

The animals were prepared by the drovers for their long, hard journey. Cows were fitted with iron shoes to protect their hooves, and geese were given leather boots. Pigs wore woollen boots fitted with leather soles on each trotter and turkeys were made to walk through a mixture of tar and sand, which would set hard on the undersides of their feet.

The drove would travel at around two miles an hour. They covered about twenty miles a day. How long would the drovers work each day?

The land where farmers fattened their pigs was called a den. Many villages in Kent have names ending in 'den', e.g. Cowden, Tenterden and Frittenden.

The return of the herd

This picture is by Pieter Bruegel the Elder. It is called *The return of the herd*, and was painted in the Middle Ages. It shows the drovers returning the cattle to their winter quarters from their summer pastures.

There was an important drovers' road that started in Rye and headed towards London. That road divided where Sevenoaks now stands, with one fork going towards London and the other going towards Dartford.

From Anglo Saxon times, shrines were built along the drovers' roads, usually where a number of the roads crossed. At the shrines, drovers and other travellers could give thanks to God and pray that the next part of their journey would be safe.

Watch out!

In Saxon times, there were WOLVES in Britain. Travellers needed somewhere safe to sleep when they were on the road.

Those using the drovers' roads would need somewhere to eat, drink and sleep when they stopped. Drovers would sleep outside to guard their animals, but if they could afford to, they might stop at an inn for food and ale. These stopping places were often close to shrines, and eventually other buildings began to appear nearby along the way.

So there you are: one reason why Sevenoaks began to develop was that it was a useful stopping place for the drovers who travelled through this part of Kent.

Traders' routes

It wasn't just the drovers who passed through the area we now know as Sevenoaks. The settlement became a useful stopping-off place for all sorts of traders and travellers journeying between London, the south coast and even as far away as Europe. Their journeys would have been long, difficult and sometimes dangerous. The tracks they used were nothing like the roads we use today; there were no drains or gullies, no hard surfaces and they were often very muddy in winter. The tracks would be very uneven and worn, and to both the north and south of Sevenoaks there were steep hills to climb.

Here is a description of the people who travelled through Sevenoaks in the Middle Ages:

'[They were] pedlars of salt from the seashore, dealers in ploughshares and ironware from the Wealden foundries, merchants of richer and more exotic goods coming from Rye and Winchelsea. Mingled with all this would be the swineherds, singly or in parties, with or without their beasts.'

From Roman times and even earlier, traders took goods such as corn, gold, silver and iron across to the Continent. Travelling in the other direction, traders from Europe imported wine, oil and glassware into Kent. Sevenoaks was a convenient place for those who wanted to break their journeys. Traders would have welcomed somewhere to stop, rest and pray, so, like the drovers, they would stop to pray at shrines to give thanks for a safe passage.

The traders give us our second reason why Sevenoaks became a settlement.

Where were the shrines?

We know exactly where some of these ancient shrines were, because many were later rebuilt and became churches. In Sevenoaks, one important shrine became St Nicholas Church at the top of the High Street.

St Nicholas Church

The first mention of Sevenoaks was in Anglo Saxon times, when the name 'Seouenaca' was given to a small shrine, or chapel, near seven large oak trees. That was over 1,200 years ago!

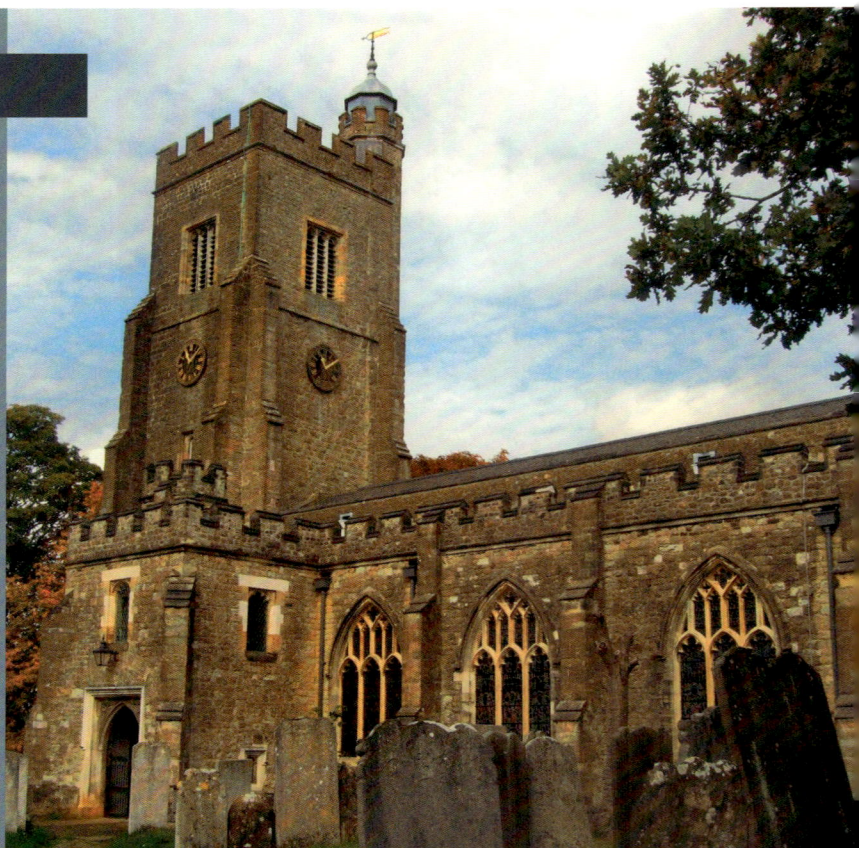

The drinking fountain in Sevenoaks where the road divides

Just a little bit further north where Sevenoaks High Street and London Road meet, there was another shrine. This area became the place where the market developed. At this point, there is now a drinking fountain. But further back in time there used to be a pond where the horses could stop for a drink of water after a very long and steep walk up the hill from the south. This steep section of road is now called 'Riverhill'. See if you can find it on a map.

There was another shrine (and a Holy Well) near the area now known as the Bat and Ball crossroads. This shrine was on the Rye road that headed north from the coast, through the Vale of Holmesdale and towards Dartford. A hospital was set up on the site in the Middle Ages, and eventually St John the Baptist Church was built further up St Johns Hill.

The fish road

The Rye Road was also known as 'the fish road' because it was used to transport baskets of fish from Rye on the Sussex coast. Packhorses took the fish to a market at Chipstead, where the fish was sold to London merchants and the Royal Court.

The market

The development of the market is our third important reason for the growth of Sevenoaks.

It wasn't until the market made Sevenoaks a successful and thriving town that it became a manor in its own right. The first written record of a market in Sevenoaks is dated 1287. However, King Henry III might have given the town a market charter even earlier, at the beginning of the thirteenth century. We know that he gave charters to a number of villages in the area at that time. Archaeological finds suggest that there might even have been a market in the town before the Norman Conquest in 1066.

Remember the tracks used by the drovers, traders and travellers?

An extra-wide high street is often a clue that it was (or still is) a market place. A Saturday market has taken place on Sevenoaks High Street for over seven hundred years.

The town started to take shape at the point where the main route from the south coast and the Weald split into two roads, heading north to London and to Dartford. The earliest Sevenoaks markets might have taken place just a short distance away at the early Saxon shrine for travellers where St Nicholas Church now stands. When deals took place in a religious building, it made them seem more trustworthy. Eventually, though, laws were passed that forbade trading on church property, so the market moved slightly further north up the road.

This area is where the town's market has taken place for centuries.

Thomas Bourchier was Archbishop of Canterbury from 1454. Because the Church looked after the Manor of Otford for the king, Archbishop Bourchier received rents from the market stall holders.

He probably built the original market house that stood at a wide area of the High Street to the north of the town. The Old Market House wasn't just used for buying and selling goods, though; it was also a court house where arguments could be sorted out and where wrongdoers could be put on trial and even sentenced to death. The Archbishop would also benefit from any fines paid at the court house.

THOMAS BOURCHIER 1454-1486

The Shambles

'The Shambles' is a medieval name for a butcher's shop or slaughterhouse. Butchers and fishmongers traded in the area between the High Street and London Road. Can you find the courtyard where this took place?

THE SHAMBLES OLD SEVENOAKS

Much later on, in 1843, a new market house was built. There were market stalls on the ground floor and there was a corn market and a coroner's court on the first floor. You can still see this building and its graceful ground-floor arches on Sevenoaks High Street; it is now used as a hairdresser's.

Sevenoaks' market flourished until the first half of the nineteenth century. Then, as the railways developed and traders took their livestock to Tonbridge and Ashford instead of Sevenoaks, it went into a decline. The weekly livestock market was moved to land opposite Sevenoaks station after the First World War but closed in 1999 to make way for a new office building.

The Sevenoaks cattle market in 1991

The weekly general market moved back into town at this point, where it still takes place on Wednesdays and Saturdays.

Why Sevenoaks' population grew

We've already worked out why Sevenoaks became a settlement. Now we need to find out why the town's population grew and what made it prosper.

In the fourteenth century, there was a range of shops in the centre of Sevenoaks, but the town was still small.

By around 1570, there were fewer than one thousand people living in Sevenoaks. The people who lived there were, in general, poor. They relied on the local market for business and on the passing trade of travellers who were on their way through town. Locals could make a living providing services such as food, lodging, drink and the stabling of horses.

Taking the waters

In the seventeenth century, it became fashionable to 'take the waters'.

In 1606, a courtier to King James I drank water from a spring in Tunbridge Wells. He had been feeling ill, and the spring water seemed to make him better. He told his rich friends about this miraculous cure. By 1630 even Queen Henrietta Maria (the wife of King Charles I) had visited the town to drink the spring water.

Many rich Londoners started to visit the newly fashionable spa town of Tunbridge Wells. These wealthy visitors stopped at Sevenoaks for a break. Don't forget that travel took a lot longer in those days, so they wouldn't do the whole journey without stopping.

Queen Henrietta Maria

They spent their money in the town and helped boost the income of the local people. By the end of the seventeenth century, with more and more rich people passing through on their way to the Tunbridge Wells spa, Sevenoaks now had enough room in its coaching inns to look after 80 travellers and 100 horses at a time.

Yuk!

The special spring water in Tunbridge Wells contains potassium, calcium, magnesium, iron and sodium. It may do you good, but it tastes HORRIBLE!

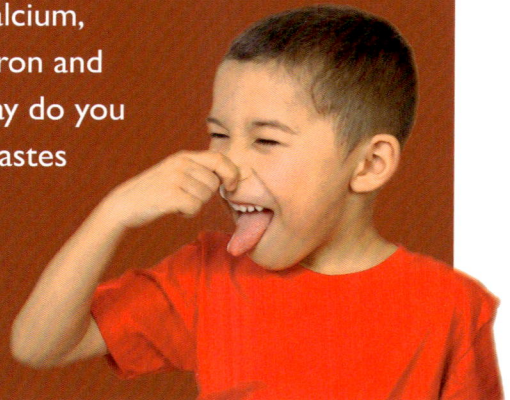

Large estates

Partly because of the number of people that passed through Sevenoaks to take the waters, Sevenoaks was suddenly on the map.

Rich people started to settle in the town.

During the eighteenth century, a number of grand houses were built, including Greatness, Bradbourne, Kippington, Wildernesse and Montreal Park. All of these great houses needed lots of servants. This, of course, meant there were more jobs for local people. All of these servants and tradespeople needed food and clothes, and they all needed somewhere to live.

Sevenoaks began to grow!

This is how Greatness Estate was described when it went on sale in 1829:

Greatness House, within one mile of Sevenoaks, containing handsome entrance hall, dining, drawing, breakfast, and music rooms, of good proportions with numerous bed rooms, double coach-house, stabling for 10 horses, green-house, ice-house, and offices of every description, with two gardens and about fifty acres of beautiful park-like land surrounding the house, with a handsome piece of water well stocked with fish.

Until the late nineteenth century, upper-class landowners lived in comfort. Their taxes were low, they earned money from farming and rents, they had political power and their servants were cheap to employ. But from around 1870, the gentry started to lose some of their power and influence in parliament and the value of their land began to fall.

All of these gardeners worked at Knole.

How old do you think the boy on the left is?

Over time, and especially after the First World War, many of the large estates around Britain went into decline. There were families who had lost their sons in battle, leaving no-one to inherit the estate. There were massive taxes (or death duties) to pay when the owner of an estate died, often leaving them without enough money to carry on running the estate. There were fewer people who were willing to work as servants, especially when there were better-paid jobs available in factories and offices, either close to home or in London.

In the 1920s, a number of Sevenoaks estate owners, including the owners of Wildernesse and Montreal Park, steadily sold off their land for housing development.

By 1955, across Britain one country house was being demolished every five days.

These houses on Wickenden Road were built in 1934.
They were some of the many built on the Wildernesse estate.

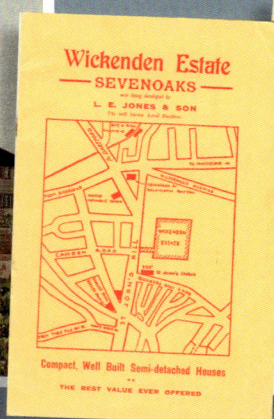

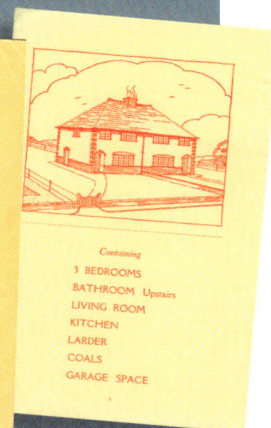

One of the last owners of Bradbourne Hall was Francis Crawshay, who bought the mansion in 1870. He built a wooden belfry and rang a huge bell at six o'clock each morning, 'to wake the lazy people of Riverhead'. It was one of the heaviest bells in the whole of the country and was so loud that it could be heard as far away as Seal!

Bradbourne Hall, Riverhead, Kent.

Economic development

In the eighteenth century, turnpike roads were introduced. These were main roads rather than tracks, and were built – and looked after – properly. Travellers had to pay to travel along them and would pay a fee at toll gates or toll houses. The turnpike roads were much easier to use than the old, muddy tracks, so journeys were faster; you could get to London from Sevenoaks in under four hours. This meant that more people used the roads, which in turn meant that more goods were traded than before. All of this was excellent news for the economy of Sevenoaks!

If you were rich enough, you could have a say in the design of your town. Heading south out of Sevenoaks along the High Street, the road suddenly turns left past Sevenoaks School. This was because Thomas Lambarde didn't want the noise and intrusion of extra traffic near his house in Sevenoaks Park. He made sure that the new Tonbridge Road turnpike that was being built wasn't sited too close to his house.

See if you can find the extra bend in the road on a map.

CLUE:
Lambarde's house, Park Place, is now a boarding house for pupils at Sevenoaks School.

Pigot's Directory of 1840 listed all the shopkeepers and traders in Sevenoaks at that time.

How many of these can you find in Sevenoaks today?

butchers	5
fishmongers	3
greengrocers	4
grocers and cheesemongers	13
wine and spirits merchants	4
hatters and clothes dealers	5
milliners and dress makers	5
hairdressers	2
linen drapers	7
tailors	8
boot and shoemakers	9
ironmongers	3
watch and clock makers	6
saddlers	3
wheelwrights	2
candle maker	1

But at the turn of the nineteenth century, Sevenoaks still only had a population of 2,600. There must have been another reason why Sevenoaks grew to the size it is today.

What could it be?

The answer is...

The railway comes to town

There wasn't just one railway company in nineteenth-century Britain. Different companies owned and developed different lines, and they competed rather than co-operated with each other.

The early railway companies didn't build a railway line to Sevenoaks. Passengers from Sevenoaks would have to travel north to St Mary Cray or south to Penshurst or Tonbridge to catch a train. In each case, they would have to begin their journey by road from Sevenoaks.

A group of local landowners worked with engineer Thomas Crampton to sort out this gap in the market by building a new railway line from Swanley to Sevenoaks (Bat and Ball). They formed the Sevenoaks Railway Company to build this new line, which was completed in 1862.

This photograph was taken at Sevenoaks Bat and Ball in around 1910. Look how many men used to work there!

The £1m railway tunnel at Sevenoaks

Soon after, the South Eastern Railway Company was given permission to extend their track from Lewisham to Tonbridge, calling at Sevenoaks on the way through. This new station became Sevenoaks (Tubs Hill), and it opened in 1868. The railway tunnel that they built at Sevenoaks was a difficult and expensive engineering project. It cost £1m and took five years to complete.

Finally, in 1869, a railway line between Tubs Hill and Bat and Ball was built. The link was complete.

It was the Sevenoaks line at Tubs Hill that proved more popular, with faster journey times to London. This made Sevenoaks a desirable place to live. Soon, new houses shops and schools were built for the families who moved to the area.

This picture of a B1 Class locomotive dates from around 1890, and was taken at Sevenoaks Bat and Ball.

So even though the population of Sevenoaks was still only 5,949 in 1871, it soon started to grow. By 1911, the population had almost doubled to 10,953 and one hundred years later it has more than doubled again to 25,000.

A little bit more about Sevenoaks

Now we know how Sevenoaks developed and prospered, let's find out some interesting facts about the town and its history.

Knole

In 1456 Thomas Bourchier, Archbishop of Canterbury, bought the Knole estate. He paid £266 13s. 4d. for the property, and turned the jumble of old buildings into a palace fit for an archbishop. He was a great builder and transformed Knole into a home where religious leaders, royalty and, eventually, the Sackville family could live in splendour.

Knole became known as a calendar house, because it had, at one time, 365 rooms, 52 staircases, 12 entrances and seven courtyards. Later on, building works altered the number of staircases in the building, so the calendar house claim to fame isn't quite true any more.

Knole House

Bourchier died at Knole in 1486. In 1538, King Henry VIII decided that he wanted the Knole estate for himself.

What the king wanted, he got!

King Henry VIII

King Henry VIII 'persuaded' Archbishop Thomas Cranmer that he should be given Otford Palace and Knole House, saying that Otford

"...standeth low and is rheumatick. As for Knole, it standeth on a sound, perfect and wholesome ground...I will live at Knole and most of my house shall live at Otford."

Henry's daughter, Elizabeth I, eventually inherited Knole. She gave the house to the Sackville family in 1577. The Sackvilles still live there, but the estate is now owned and managed by the National Trust.

St Nicholas Church

St Nicholas

St Nicholas is one of the most popular Christian saints, with more than 400 churches dedicated to him in England alone. He is the patron saint of sailors and travellers. Perhaps you recognise the name for a different reason, though: he is also the patron saint of children and is known as Santa Claus!

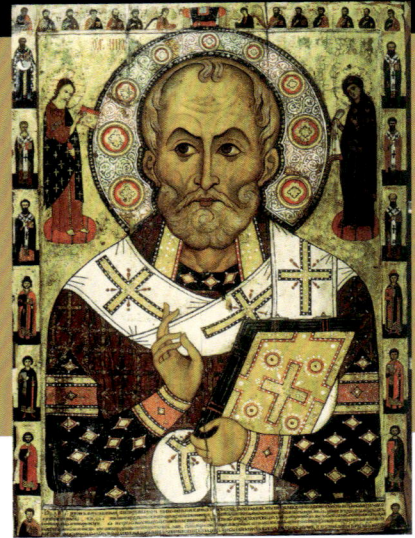

First there was just a wayside shrine for travellers passing through the area.

Then came a stone building – probably the only one in Sevenoaks at the time. This small church is mentioned in records from the time of King Henry I (1100–1135) and would have been much smaller than the church we know today.

In 1320, the church was enlarged. By this date there was a regular market taking place there.

Features such as the 90ft tower, the south aisle and the chancel weren't added until the middle of the fifteenth century. It's likely that Archbishop Bourchier was responsible for enlarging St Nicholas Church, when he lived over the road at Knole.

Sevenoaks School

Sevenoaks School became a free grammar school for boys because of the generosity of a poor orphan called William Sevenoke. The landowner who fostered the young boy didn't know his surname, so he was named after the town.

William Sevenoke

William Sevenoke became Lord Mayor of London in 1418. The person who followed him as London's lord mayor was Dick Whittington.

When he died in 1432, William Sevenoke was a rich man. He wrote six wills, leaving most of his money to churches in London. But he made sure that some of the property he owned in London would pay for new school buildings in Sevenoaks, and for almshouses for the poor. This was his way of thanking the town where he grew up.

In 1560, the school became 'Queen Elizabeth's Grammar School' when Queen Elizabeth I granted special status to the school. The document she signed was a sort of royal proclamation, called 'Letters Patent'. They can still be granted by the monarch today.

Sevenoaks School was established 'for the education of boys and youths in grammar and learning'. Girls weren't allowed to attend the school until 1976. That's 544 years after the school started!

The seven oaks

So where was the first group of seven oaks?

We know that Sevenoaks town was named after a group of oak trees. An early shrine from Saxon times was given the name 'Seouanaca' because of the seven great oaks that stood nearby. Some think that they may have been growing in what became the Manor of Knole Park as long ago as 800AD.

Groups of oaks have been planted at different times, usually to celebrate a particular event, such as a coronation. Seven oaks were planted in the eighteenth century on the Tonbridge road to the south of Sevenoaks, but they were replaced in the 1950s. The oak trees in Knole Park have been replaced several times over the centuries.

In 1902 seven oaks were planted on the north side of the Vine cricket ground to commemorate the coronation of King Edward VII. During the Great Storm of 1987, six of the Vine trees were blown down. Replacement trees were planted but were vandalised, leaving just one mature tree standing. The other six trees were again replaced and eight oak trees now grow along the edge of the Vine.

The town's motto is *Floreant Septum Quercus* – *May the seven oaks flourish*. The town's coat of arms includes seven gold acorns.

Can you see the Y shape?

This is to remind us of that important London and Dartford road junction where the town first developed.

No. A hurricane needs sea surface temperatures of 27°C or more, and tropical moisture to feed upon. We don't get these conditions in Britain. The Great Storm was just a very powerful storm. There may not be another storm like it for another 200 years!

The Great Storm

When Sevenoaks was hit by the full force of the Great Storm in October 1987, people around the world began to joke that the town should be called 'One Oak'. They didn't know that there are lots of groups of seven oaks around the town. The oaks that most people knew about were the symbolic seven oaks on the Vine, six of which were blown down in the storm.

It was the town's position high up on the Greensand Ridge that led to so much damage taking place in Sevenoaks. One million trees blew down across the Sevenoaks District, including 70% of the trees in Knole Park. Power lines came down, houses were destroyed and 900 miles of roads around the District were blocked by fallen trees.

The Vine cricket ground

The Vine cricket ground is one of the oldest cricket venues in the country. It's thought that it might once have been a small vineyard owned by the Archbishop of Canterbury. That's how this piece of land got its name.

By 1734, the land was very neglected. The owner, John Frederick Sackville, the third duke of Dorset, was a keen cricketer and he turned the Vine into a cricket pitch. He decided to give the land to the town of Sevenoaks. It was agreed that the Vine Cricket Club would pay a rent of two peppercorns a year to the town – one for the ground and one for the pavilion that had been built. These days, the club pays the Town Council for the upkeep of the land. They also have to pay a rental fee of one cricket ball a year to the current Lord Sackville, if asked.

The Vine cricket ground in 1780

Cricket

As the game became more and more popular around the country, a new industry was created. Cricket bats and balls were made in Sevenoaks for the players who had taken up this new sport.

Peppercorn rent

The term 'peppercorn rent' is still used today, to mean a very small amount of money paid to rent something (usually land or a property).

During the First World War, the Vine cricket pitch became a parade ground, and the Vine Pavilion was used as a canteen for the troops.

The workhouse

Did you know that Sevenoaks once had a workhouse?

No-one went there by choice; it was a last resort as the conditions were made deliberately horrible to discourage people from going there. Parents were separated from their children, and boys were separated from girls.

Many Victorians thought that poor people were lazy. Some rich families tried to help the poor, by visiting families in need to give them food and medicines.

But if there was no work available or the grown-ups were too ill to work, it was all too easy for a family to run out of money. Imagine being so poor that you had no food to eat, no warm clothes to wear and nowhere to live!

Oliver Twist

Charles Dickens wrote about an orphan who was sent to the workhouse in *Oliver Twist*. Dickens himself knew what it was like to be poor. When he was a child his own family ended up in a debtors' prison. This was even worse than life in the workhouse, but at least the family was allowed to stay together in the prison.

Children from poor families had to work from around the age of seven years old, to help their families earn enough money to get by. Some Sevenoaks children worked at the silk mill at Greatness. Many worked on farms. Others worked as chimney sweeps or were put to work making items at home.

At least in the workhouse they learnt reading, writing and arithmetic. The boys were trained for a trade and the girls were taught sewing and housework so that they could become domestic servants. They would wear a special uniform to show that they were workhouse children, and that they were the poorest of the poor.

The Sevenoaks parish workhouse on St John's Hill was built in the 1730s. Even when it was extended there were still too many people living there. By 1841 there were 347 people in a building designed for 300. The Poor Law Commissioners wrote a report about the conditions they found there when they inspected the workhouse. Four boys slept in each bed, the blankets were very thin and the meat puddings they were given to eat were 'an indigestible form of food'. *The Times* reported that the poor conditions were a scandal, and eventually a bigger, Union workhouse was built in Sundridge instead.

St John's Hill was often referred to as 'Workhouse Hill' in the past.

The workhouse kitchen at Sundridge

By the end of the eighteenth century there were nearly 2,000 parish workhouses in Britain. From 1834, parish workhouses were grouped into unions. Larger, union workhouses – like this one in Sundridge – were built, replacing the smaller workhouses like Sevenoaks.

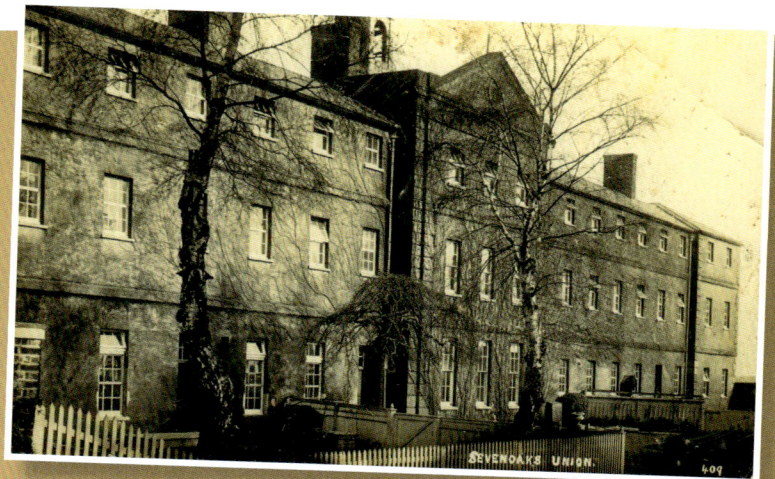

Famous people with Sevenoaks connections

H G Wells (1866–1946)

The author H G Wells lived at 23 Eardley Road, Sevenoaks in 1894. He finished writing *The Time Machine* at this address. H G Wells wrote many other science fiction novels, including *The Invisible Man*, *The War of the Worlds*, *The First Men in the Moon* and *The Shape of Things to Come*. Many of his books have been made into films.

Diana, Princess of Wales (1961–1997)

As a schoolgirl, Diana attended West Heath School, a girls' boarding school in Sevenoaks. In 1981, she married Prince Charles. Their wedding at St Paul's Cathedral was watched by over 750 million people. As Princess of Wales, she often represented the Queen at official functions, and was a great favourite of the public. Her fashionable dress sense and charity work made her famous all over the world. Prince Charles and Diana, Princess of Wales had two sons – Prince William and Prince Harry – but were divorced in 1996.

Diana died in a car accident in Paris on 31st August 1997.

West Heath School

W H Davies (1871–1940)

After a hard life as a tramp, W H Davies became famous as a poet. Born in South Wales, Davies first worked for an ironmonger and then as an apprentice picture frame maker, but he was restless and dreamt of travelling and making a fortune. He left his job and travelled across the Atlantic Ocean to America, finding work wherever he could. He then went to seek his fortune in Canada after reading about the gold rush in the Klondike. On his way there, he tried to jump onto a train for a free ride. His foot was crushed under the wheel of the train, and his leg was eventually amputated below the knee.

Returning to Britain, he spent many rough nights in hostels in London. In order to make some money, he secretly wrote poems and tried to sell them. Luckily for him, a publisher eventually discovered these poems, and Davies' life started to improve. He moved to Sevenoaks and, over the next seven years, lived at a number of addresses around the town before moving to London, where he made many literary friends.

He wrote a famous poem called 'Leisure', which starts:

"What is this life if, full of care,

We have no time to stand and stare.

No time to stand beneath the boughs

And stare as long as sheep or cows.

No time to see, when woods we pass,

Where squirrels hide their nuts in grass...."

This poem warns us that we live life too quickly, and that our lives would be better if we took time to enjoy the natural world.

Jane Austen (1775–1817)

Jane Austen was an English author. Her books show what life was like for nineteenth-century middle- and upper-class people, and for women in particular. There have been many versions of her books on the big screen and on television.

The books she wrote, which include *Sense and Sensibility, Pride and Prejudice* and *Emma*, were all published anonymously. At the time, it wasn't 'ladylike' for women to publish books for money.

Jane visited Sevenoaks in 1788, aged 12. She stayed at the Red House, with her mother, father and her sister Cassandra. The Red House was owned by her great uncle, Francis, who also bought Kippington House in 1796.

Vita Sackville-West (1892–1962)

Vita Sackville-West was a novelist, a poet and a garden designer. She was born at Knole, and some of her stories were set in Knole House and in the town of Sevenoaks. When her father died, she couldn't inherit Knole because she was a woman. She was very disappointed about this. Instead, her uncle, Charles, inherited the property.

Eventually, Vita and her husband bought Sissinghurst Castle near Cranbrook in Kent. Over the years, they rebuilt this derelict property and redesigned the gardens together. Sissinghurst Castle is now owned by the National Trust and draws visitors from all over the world to see its beautiful landscaped gardens.

Even today, women from noble families can't inherit their father's title or land, even if they are the eldest child. Instead, the closest male relative becomes the heir.

The Beatles

The Beatles were a 1960s' rock group from Liverpool. There were four people in the group: John Lennon, Paul McCartney, George Harrison and Ringo Starr. In 1967, The Beatles came to Knole Park in Sevenoaks to make promotional films for two of their songs, *Strawberry Fields Forever* and *Penny Lane*. Some say that these films were the first-ever pop music promotional videos.

Beatles fans still come to Knole Park to see where the filming took place. They look for a particular oak tree near the Bird House where the Beatles filmed. But the oak tree was already dead when the Beatles made their film, and is no longer there.

Books about Sevenoaks

You will find these books, and many more, at Sevenoaks Library

HARPER, Russell *Sevenoaks and around through time.*
Amberley, 2013. ISBN 978 1445618371
This book shows old views of Sevenoaks and compares them with photographs of Sevenoaks as it is today.

KILLINGRAY, David and PURVES, Elizabeth (eds.) *Sevenoaks: An Historical Dictionary.*
Phillimore, 2012. ISBN 978 1860777363
This book is currently out of print but a free download is available on the internet. Go to www.sevenoakshistory.org.uk and click on 'Resources'. Everything you need to know about the historical buildings, the people and the events of Sevenoaks is included in this alphabetical list of entries.

OGLEY, Bob *In the wake of the hurricane.*
Froglets, 1987. ISBN 0 95130190X
Pictures and first-hand accounts of the night of the Great Storm.

SHELTON, Rod *Darent: the history and stories of a river and its communities.*
Stanhope, 2015. ISBN 978 0950396392
Lots of information, history and pictures about all the villages and towns along the Darent Valley.

THOMPSON, Ed and CLUCAS, Philip *Sevenoaks St Johns – the past in pictures.*
Hopgarden, 2013. ISBN 978 0950396385
130 interesting photographs of old Sevenoaks and its residents. One of a series by these authors.

How to find out more

As well as lots of pictures, Sevenoaks Library has more information that you could include in your project.

- If your house is over one hundred years old, you can see who used to live there.
- If you want to find out about your family, you can use a library computer to look at some family history records.
- You can look at old newspapers, using a microfilm reader.
- You can hunt through the library files to look at things like programmes and magazine clippings.

Some of these records are quite difficult to understand, so take a grown up with you!

There is a museum in the library, too. You can watch a film about the market and look at interesting items connected with the town.

You could also ask some local people for their memories of old Sevenoaks.

How to make your project look good

Sevenoaks Library has lots of pictures, maps and drawings of the town. If you want to use them for a school project, go and talk to the lovely staff there. They will help you find suitable pictures for your project and will help you to photocopy them.

You can have up to five free photocopies or printouts a day if it's for your homework.

Unbelievable!

Picture credits and acknowledgements

Thank you to everyone who took the time to look through the text of this book as I was writing it, in particular Elizabeth Purves and Ed Thompson.

Many of the pictures that I used in this book belong to other people. I'd like to thank these individuals and organisations for letting me use the images, and below are the relevant acknowledgements.

The Shambles sculpture images on the cover and elsewhere in the book are by Juliet Simpson www.jssculptures.co.uk

Deer in front of Knole Park
By David Anstiss; licensed under the Creative Commons Attribution-ShareAlike 4.0 Generic Licence.

Lullingstone Roman Villa
Licensed under the Creative Commons License Attribution – Generic dissemination Alike 3.0

Model of Otford's Archbishop's Palace
Reproduced by kind permission of Rod Shelton

Archbishop's Palace ruins
By Richard Croft; licensed for reuse under the Creative Commons Attribution-ShareAlike 2.0 license

Hampton Court main entrance gatehouse
By Torecles. This file is licensed under the Creative Commons Attribution-Share Alike 3.0

Drover road and **Girl herding pigs**
Reproduced by kind permission of High Weald AONB. Find out more about the region's medieval landscape at www.highweald.org

St Nicholas Church, Sevenoaks
cc-by-sa/2.0 – © Paul Gillett -geograph.org.uk/p/2614164

Knole House
By John Wilder; licensed under CC by 4.0

Sevenoaks Town crest
Reproduced by kind permission of Sevenoaks Town Council. This image must not be reproduced without permission from Sevenoaks Town Council.

West Heath School
© Copyright Jean Barrow and licensed for reuse under the Creative Commons Attribution-ShareAlike 2.0 licence BY-SA 2.0

I would like to thank Ed Thompson, in particular, for his generosity; the following images are *all* reproduced with his kind permission:

- Holmesdale Valley at Sundridge
- Sevenoaks cattle market pictures
- Kippington House
- Wickenden Road images
- Bradbourne Hall postcard
- Railway station pictures
- Sevenoaks Bat and Ball with staff
- The Sevenoaks tunnel
- The B1 Class locomotive
- The Great Storm pictures
- The Vine in the 1970s
- Sevenoaks Union workhouse kitchen
- Sevenoaks Union workhouse

The following images were purchased from Fotolia image library:

page 5 (top), © voren1; page 10, © ilyaska; page 12 (bottom), © Mickeing; pages 13 and 21 (bottom), © Andrey Kuzmin; page 15 (bottom), © ssshy; page 25, © LiliGraphie; page 35 (top), © mgp; pages 38, 39 and 40 (frames), © JackF

Finally, my greatest thanks go to Patricia Briggs, who designed, proof read and edited this book for me. If you're thinking of writing your own book, get in touch with her, and you'll end up with a book that looks as lovely as this one!

PATRICIA BRIGGS DESIGN, EDITING AND PROJECT MANAGEMENT
01959 526864 • patriciabriggs@fastmail.com • uk.linkedin.com/in/patriciabriggsdesign